WILLIAM GRANT STILL
African-American Composer

WILLIAM GRANT STILL
African-American Composer

Catherine Reef

MORGAN
REYNOLDS
Publishing, Inc.

620 South Elm Street, Suite 223
Greensboro, North Carolina 27406
http://www.morganreynolds.com

WILLIAM GRANT STILL: AFRICAN-AMERICAN COMPOSER

Library of Congress Cataloging-in-Publication Data

Reef, Catherine.
    William Grant Still : African-American composer / Catherine Reef.
        p. cm. -- (Masters of music)
Summary: Traces the life of the African American classical composer.
Includes bibliographical references (p.   ) and index.
    ISBN 1-931798-11-7 (library binding)
    1. Still, William Grant, 1895---Juvenile literature. 2.
Composers--United States--Biography--Juvenile literature. 3.   African
American composers--Biography--Juvenile literature. [1. Still, William
Grant, 1895- 2. Composers. 3. African Americans--Biography.] I. Title.
II. Masters of music (Greensboro, N.C.)
    ML3930.S78R4 2003
    780'.92--dc21

                            2003002231

Masters of Music

William Grant Still

John Coltrane

George Gershwin

Shinichi Suzuki

Bix Beiderbecke

. . . nothing ever is; it is always becoming.
—*William Grant Still*

Contents

William Grant Still.
(Courtesy of the Library of Congress.)

Chapter One

The Teacher's Child

Little David, play on your harp,
Hallelu', Hallelu',
Little David, play on your harp,
Hallelu' . . .

Anne Fambro often sang spirituals while she cooked and cleaned the house. They were songs she had learned many years earlier while growing up in slavery in Georgia. Now it was 1903, and she was a free woman living in Little Rock, Arkansas.

Her eight-year-old grandson sat nearby, his books spread out on the desk in the parlor. Young William Grant Still was supposed to be studying. His mother had told him again and again he "*must* amount to something in the world." She planned for him to go to college and become a doctor, a man worthy of her pride. When his grandmother sang, though, Will felt compelled to stop working and listen.

Even in childhood, music spoke directly to his soul. Its message proved so strong that William Grant Still grew up to compose music of his own. Through persistence, he would succeed as a black composer in the world of serious music, which was dominated by whites.

In the first half of the twentieth century, when William Grant Still composed his most important works, many people expected black musicians to write and perform popular songs, spirituals, jazz, and the blues—and nothing else. Orchestras often declined to play works by black composers.

Over the course of a long career, Still would complete approximately two hundred musical works, including symphonies, operas, and ballets, many of them inspired by events in African-American history. He focused on African-American themes in order to bring people together. He was convinced racism resulted from ignorance and that his music increased understanding. "When we all awaken to the fact that each group has something important and worthwhile to contribute to the culture of the entire country," he said, "then we will have a society that is well integrated—in which all of us will be working for the common good."

Will began learning about African-American history in childhood, hearing his grandmother recall the days of slavery. She described African Americans chained together and marching to the slave market where they would be sold, and the overseer who whipped anyone walking too slowly. It was a scene Fambro would never forget.

Still's Grandmother Anne Fambro was a former slave whose singing of spirituals helped inspire her grandson's love of music. *(Courtesy of the University of Arkansas.)*

Will, in turn, read his grandmother the detective stories and Western novels that she loved. Like most enslaved people, Anne Fambro had never learned to read. She kept the books hidden in her closet because Will's mother disapproved of them. Carrie Still instructed her son to read books by Horatio Alger, who wrote about boys working hard and achieving success, and classics such as *Gulliver's Travels*.

Will's mother loved the world of learning, even as a girl. Carrie Fambro attended Atlanta University and trained to be a teacher, graduating in 1886. In 1894, she married a fellow student, William Grant Still Sr., who was a teacher as well. The couple settled in Still's hometown of Woodville, Mississippi, and on May 11, 1895, William Grant Still Jr. was born.

Will's mother, Carrie Still, was a school teacher. She encouraged her son to become a doctor. *(Courtesy of the University of Arkansas.)*

Baby Will was never to know his father. When the child was three months old, William Grant Still Sr. grew sick. No one could say with certainty what had made him ill. Some people said it was typhoid, caused by drinking contaminated water; others insisted it was malaria, transmitted by a mosquito. There were also whisperings of witchcraft. African tales of spirits in animal form—stories carried to North America by slaves—

lived on in the Mississippi woods. Carrie Still told of a spooky owl that had perched on their roof throughout her husband's illness and only flew away when he died.

Newly widowed, Carrie Still took her infant son to Little Rock, where her mother and sister lived. She found a job teaching English at Little Rock's high school for African Americans and soon bought a house. Her mother looked after Will while she worked.

At the turn of the twentieth century, Little Rock was a segregated city. Black and white children attended separate schools, and African Americans traveling by train had to ride in designated cars. The public library, with its thirty-two hundred books, was for whites only.

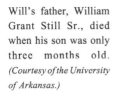

Will's father, William Grant Still Sr., died when his son was only three months old. *(Courtesy of the University of Arkansas.)*

In 1903, the municipal government passed a law requiring segregation on the city's streetcars.

Some whites went beyond the law to remind African Americans of their second-class status. As a child, Will saw a white police officer beat a black man on Little Rock's Center Street until the man's blood covered the sidewalk. That scene "horrified me," Still said, "but did not change my feeling that the good people in Little Rock overbalanced the bad."

Although she could do nothing to stop racial violence, Carrie Still worked to improve life for the thirty-eight percent of Little Rock's citizens who were black. She spent hours after school helping some of her former students present plays by William Shakespeare to raise money for a library for Little Rock's African Americans. Carrie Still taught her son that he was "an American, in the finest sense of the word," and that "he must never let anyone take away his humanity with a label." She raised him in a racially mixed neighborhood, so that he would have friends among blacks and whites.

Will and the other boys were constantly getting into mischief. They played with matches, and they skipped school to watch freight trains pass by. Once, they poured water on a teacher's chair before he sat down. Will knew he would receive a whipping if his mother learned about his role in these pranks. Carrie Still was certain that without harsh punishment, her son would follow "the path of least resistance."

"She had an educated whipping strap," laughed a grown-up William Grant Still, who tried never to criti-

Baby Will grew up in the segregated city of Little Rock, Arkansas. *(Courtesy of the University of Arkansas.)*

cize anyone. "If I crawled under the bed to escape, the strap curled under ahead of me."

Sometimes Will liked to play by himself or work with his hands. He was always making things, such as toy cannons and miniature roller coasters. He built toy violins of smooth, varnished wood and fitted them with tiny strings that produced musical notes when plucked.

Because the building that housed Will's elementary school contained the high school as well, his mother kept a close watch on him throughout the school day. She made sure that he did his homework and earned good grades, and she insisted he eat lunch with her every noon before running out to the schoolyard to play.

When Carrie Still traveled to rural Arkansas one summer to teach poor African-American children, she brought Will along. At home, Will had many books, and he was surprised the boys and girls he met on this trip owned none. These children went to school only in summer because their community could not afford a full-time teacher. Instead of a roof, their school had a covering of tree branches that let in rain and insects alike.

One Sunday, the townspeople invited Carrie and Will to a church service and picnic. Will had heard spirituals sung by his grandmother at home, but this was the first time he heard them performed in a country church. "The thought that I was 'hearing authentic Negro music at its source' never entered my irreverent little mind," Still noted. To him, the singing was "a hilarious show put on just for my benefit." When the congregation began to chant, clap, and stamp their feet, Will threw back his head and laughed for joy—until his mother scolded him and sent him outside.

During other summers, Will and his grandmother, Anne Fambro, rode a train to Georgia to visit cousins who lived there. One hazy day, as they sat on their relatives' porch, they saw white men armed with rifles step out of some nearby woods. Will asked his grandmother what the men were doing, and she explained that a black man had been accused of a crime and had gone into hiding. The whites were part of a lynch mob, an army of local citizens intent on punishing the man without a lawful trial.

Punishment at the hands of a lynch mob almost always meant torture and death. There were about twenty-five hundred lynchings in the American South between 1885 and 1900, and they continued to occur in the early twentieth century. Nearly all of the victims were African American, and many were innocent. Whether the Georgia lynch mob that Will saw ever found the accused man is unknown, but the sight of those armed, hate-driven farmers remained in Still's memory for life.

November 15, 1905, was another memorable day. On that date, Booker T. Washington spoke to three thousand people at Little Rock's Opera House. African Americans traveled many miles to see the great man and hear what he had to say. Washington, who was born in slavery, had become a leading spokesperson for black America. Since 1881, he had directed the Tuskegee Institute, a vocational school for African Americans that was located in Alabama. Washington taught that African Americans had to work their way up slowly in society, to achieve equality step by step. He counseled young blacks to learn useful trades and put their muscles to work. Later generations could employ their minds and be the writers, scientists, and scholars of their race. He told the audience in Little Rock, "There is little or no opposition of prejudice to the Negro laborer in the South, and it is my greatest concern that the people take advantage of their opportunities."

Other influential African Americans spoke out against

Students in the workshop of the Tuskegee Institute in 1920.
(Courtesy of the Library of Congress.)

Washington and his teachings. The chief critic was
W.E.B. Du Bois, a professor at Atlanta University who
later helped to found the National Association for the
Advancement of Colored People (NAACP). Du Bois
wanted the brightest ten percent of young blacks—
those he called the "Talented Tenth"—to have the best
education possible. Only through education could they
become the new leaders of the African-American community.

When Will was eleven, his mother married one of

Little Rock's outstanding African Americans. Charles B. Shepperson was a railway postal clerk with a fine mind who loved music and the theater. Whenever cultured African-American musicians performed in Little Rock, he made sure that Will heard them. Will and his parents were present when the concert singer E. Azalia Hackley gave a recital in Little Rock. Madame Hackley performed throughout the United States to raise money for scholarships for African-American students. They also heard a program by Clarence Cameron White, who was just beginning a long career as a violinist, composer, and teacher.

Will and his stepfather attended musical shows written by Bob Cole, a performer and songwriter, and J.

Born into slavery, Booker T. Washington became the director of Tuskegee Institute, an outspoken leader in the black community, and a strong influence on young Will. *(Courtesy of the Library of Congress.)*

Charles B. Shepperson imparted his love of music and theater to his stepson, Will. *(Courtesy of the University of Arkansas.)*

Rosamond Johnson, a classically trained pianist. Cole and Johnson created shows with African-American characters who displayed intelligence and a wide range of emotions. Previously, African Americans had been portrayed on the American stage as simple-minded, humorous folk. *The Shoo-Fly Regiment,* a Cole and Johnson show produced in 1907, dealt with African-American soldiers serving in the Spanish-American War of 1898. *The Red Moon* (1909) had both African-American and Native American characters.

When phonographs became popular in the early 1900s, Charles Shepperson bought one and brought it home. He also began to collect recordings of the great singers of Europe and the United States. Those early records sounded tinny, but they introduced Will to opera, and he was enchanted. All at once he knew he wanted to be a musician and to compose operas of his own one day. He began to take violin lessons, and soon he was making manuscript paper for composing by drawing sets of five straight lines across each page for musical notation.

To Carrie Shepperson, music lessons were part of a well-rounded education, but she insisted Will devote equal time to his schoolwork. This was especially true when he entered high school and was a student in his mother's English class. His schoolmates expected him to be the teacher's pet, but instead of making things easier for her son, Mrs. Shepperson demanded more from him than she did from the others. His behavior had

Still (*top row, third from left*) spoke at the graduation of his high school class in 1911.
(Courtesy of the University of Arkansas.)

to be perfect. If he giggled in class or answered a question incorrectly, she gave him a sharp smack with her ruler. The other students soon felt sorry for the teacher's child.

Will grew to be a slender young man with delicate features who wore his dark hair neatly parted on the side. His large eyes told the world if he felt happy, angry, or wistful. When he finished high school in 1911, he had the best grades in the senior class and was invited to speak at graduation. His mother was so thrilled that it almost seemed as if she were the one selected. She taught Will how to address a crowd and how to stand and move on stage. She also wrote his speech and took away his violin until he had memorized the words.

Carrie Shepperson had decided after graduation, Will would attend Wilberforce University in Ohio and prepare for a career in medicine. She was stunned when her son announced he had a different career in mind, and it was neither medicine nor music. Inspired by Booker T. Washington, Will said he was going to raise chickens.

Chapter Two

Nothing but Music

A chicken farmer! Was the son of Carrie Still Shepperson going to spend his life chasing hens and roosters? Not if she could help it. Will's mother pleaded and argued with him until she persuaded him to give up that plan. She breathed a big sigh of relief in the fall of 1911 when sixteen-year-old Will entered Wilberforce University in Ohio. There, he began a course of study that was to prepare him to enter medical school and take his place among the "Talented Tenth."

Wilberforce University was founded in 1856 as a college for blacks. Named for William Wilberforce, an English statesman and abolitionist of the eighteenth century, the school was affiliated with the African Methodist Episcopal Church. Like Atlanta University in Georgia and Howard University in Washington, D.C., Wilberforce was one of several colleges that had been established in the nineteenth century to educate African Americans. Many other universities refused to accept black students or admitted them only in very small numbers.

The school had been erected in a picturesque region of forests, springs, and streams. Its buildings stood near the edge of a cliff overlooking Massey's Creek, which meandered toward the Little Miami River, three miles away. "No more beautiful or suitable place for the environment of young people seeking culture of mind and heart, could have been found on the earth," wrote the Reverend Horace Talbert, secretary of the university's board of trustees, in 1906.

Students came to Wilberforce from every state in the nation, as well as the Caribbean Islands, South America, and Africa. Whether the students agreed with the educational ideas of W.E.B. Du Bois or Booker T. Washington, Wilberforce had something to offer each of them.

Will attended Wilberforce University in order to prepare for medical school.
(Courtesy of the Library of Congress.)

Still *(holding violin case)* spent most of his time at Wilberforce developing his musical talents and playing music with fellow students. *(Courtesy of the University of Arkansas.)*

Many students worked toward degrees in the sciences, classical languages and literature, theology, business, and art. Others sought vocational training, wishing to be teachers, secretaries, cooks, printers, or carpenters.

In addition, Wilberforce was the only college for African Americans that required young men to undergo military training. Through marching in uniforms and learning to follow orders and handle weapons, "patriotism is more staunchly developed in the breasts of the young cadets," stated the Reverend Talbert. "And, secondly, the daily drill gives an erectness of carriage and elegance of bearing that distinguishes the student throughout life."

College students sometimes learn important lessons outside the classroom. Living on their own, away from home and family, they learn about themselves and about life. At Wilberforce, William discovered how much music mattered to him. There were so many opportunities to play and hear music on campus and in the nearby city of Dayton that he had little time left for studying. An outstanding student in high school, he earned only average grades in college.

Will and three other students formed a string quartet, and Will arranged music for the group. That is, he rewrote familiar songs so that they might be played on two violins, a viola, and a cello, which were the instruments in the quartet.

Will hated to pass up any chance to make music. When he heard the university was forming a band, he signed up to be the clarinetist—and then learned to play the clarinet from a book. Soon the bandleader left Wilberforce, and Will took over that job. As the group's leader, he needed to know how to play all of the different band instruments, so he practiced on them at night, marching in the hall outside his dormitory room. The professor who supervised the dormitory lived in the building as well, and William's constant practicing drove him crazy. Night after night, he threw open his door to shout, "Are you at it again?" Will would then hurry to his bed, slide under the blankets, and pretend to sleep.

Years later, when William Grant Still was a famous man, his college teachers claimed they had recognized his greatness while he was a student. Still joked, "They certainly didn't think I was great when I was learning to play the oboe up and down their halls!"

Will accepted every opportunity to play music. He is seated at the far right with the Wilberforce University string quartet. *(Courtesy of the University of Arkansas.)*

Young Will also arranged songs for the band. Once, when he wanted an arrangement to include the sounds of a piccolo, he learned to play that instrument himself and taught it to another student. In the same way, he mastered the saxophone so he could teach a band member to play it and feature it in his arrangements. He also composed music, and when the band performed his songs in a campus concert, the audience responded with applause and praise.

Will returned home from school on vacation to announce he had made an important decision. He was going to leave Wilberforce, give up the study of medicine, and enter the Oberlin Conservatory, a renowned school of music in northern Ohio. "I *must* become a composer," he said.

Carrie Shepperson was stunned. She told her son that if he went to Oberlin, he would be throwing away his future. She said it was impossible for a black person, including one with real talent, to succeed in the world of serious music, which was dominated by whites.

Will pointed out some black musicians who had gained recognition in that world. Clarence Cameron White, the violinist and composer, had spent two years in London, studying and performing. White, who practiced for his concert tours at the Oberlin Conservatory, had recently visited Wilberforce and praised Still's compositions. Will also mentioned Samuel Coleridge-Taylor, son of an African father and an English mother. Coleridge-Taylor was conductor of the London Handel Society and had toured the United States three times— in 1904, 1906, and 1910—conducting his own compositions. Finally, Will reminded his mother of the lesson he had learned in childhood from the books by Horatio Alger: With hard work, anyone can succeed in the United States of America.

Carrie Shepperson remained unconvinced. Even with the finest conservatory training, she feared Will would spend his life in saloons, playing "immoral" music like ragtime and the blues, and living a life of drunkenness. She worried that as a barroom musician he would be unwelcome in the homes of educated and cultured people.

Reluctantly, Will returned to Wilberforce and the

Samuel Coleridge-Taylor, whose father was African and his mother English, became a classical composer and conductor in England. *(Courtesy of the Library of Congress.)*

study of science, but music's pull proved too hard to resist. He used his allowance to buy books about the world's great symphonies and the scores, or sheet music, for operas. He pored over these works instead of his textbooks, and when he was not reading about music, he was composing it. "And so I wasted time in college just barely making my grades," Still admitted, "always in trouble for playing pranks; spending most of my time studying music, attempting to write and playing my violin." Now, when he went home on vacation, he waited until his parents were asleep to compose in his pajamas at the dining-room table.

As a beginning composer, he experimented with different ways of working. Once, he tried writing music in the Ohio woods after reading that Ludwig van Beethoven liked to compose surrounded by nature. Will found, though, that instead of focusing on music, his mind kept wandering to a patch of wild strawberries growing nearby. From then on, he did all of his composing indoors.

He eagerly submitted his work to competitions, hoping to win prizes and recognition, but the judges always sent his compositions back. Although the work showed promise, the judges commented that Will had much more to learn before his music would merit a prize.

In the spring of 1915, William Grant Still left Wilberforce University. Graduation was only two months away, and he had already purchased his cap and gown. The events surrounding his departure are unclear. It is known he was one of several students, male and female, who stayed out late one night against school rules, but university officials viewed the offense as minor, and he was not punished. Most likely, Will simply knew he would be miserable practicing medicine. "Nothing but music would do," he said. He put aside for the present his dream of attending the Oberlin Conservatory, packed up his clothes, his violin, and his oboe, and looked for a way to earn his living as a musician.

His first job was in a pool hall in Columbus, Ohio, where he cleaned billiard balls and set them up for players, earning six dollars a week. Before long, he was hired to play oboe and cello in an orchestra at Luna Park, a Cleveland, Ohio, amusement park.

Crowds flocked to Luna Park for its rides, exhibits,

Still's first paying job as a musician was at Luna Park in Cleveland, Ohio.
(Courtesy of the Library of Congress)

and entertainment. The park offered circus stars, such as James E. Hardy, "King of the Wire," who had crossed Niagara Falls on a tightrope sixteen times in the summer of 1896. Audiences also enjoyed vaudeville shows featuring comedians, musicians, and acrobats, and there was exotic entertainment, such as DeKreke's Mysterious Asia, a show with whirling dervishes, magicians, and dancing girls. Most popular of all were the band and orchestra concerts presented four times a day in summer.

In his free time, Will got together with other orches-

Shortly after her marriage to Will, Grace Bundy returned to live with her parents in Danville, Kentucky. *(Cloud's Studio.)*

tra members to play classical music, and he attended many concerts. Yet although he was living a musician's life, he was lonely. He began to exchange letters with a young woman he had known at Wilberforce named Grace Bundy. The two quickly became close friends, and on October 4, 1915, they married.

Once again, an angry Carrie Shepperson insisted Will had made a serious mistake. This time, it appeared she was correct. Grace seemed more attached to her parents than to her new husband. In the spring of 1916, pregnant with the couple's first child, she went to live with her parents in Danville, Kentucky. There were no jobs for musicians in Danville, so Will stayed in Cleveland. Alone again, he sought comfort in faith. He promised himself if he ever succeeded as a composer, he would use his talent to serve God. Toward the end of his life, Still wrote, "This was a promise which I made in my own way, and which—also in my own way—I have kept."

Chapter Three

Restless

From the nightclubs of Cleveland, a mournful song spilled into the streets: "I hate to see that evenin' sun go down."

In cities throughout the United States and Europe, people were playing this haunting tune in nightspots and on phonographs. Thousands had bought the sheet music and were sounding it out on parlor pianos. Published in 1914, "The St. Louis Blues," by W.C. Handy, had quickly become one of the most popular songs ever written. Its success had made bandleader William Christopher Handy, the son of emancipated slaves, one of the most celebrated African-American musicians of his time.

Before Handy began publishing his compositions in 1910, blues songs were stored in musicians' memories and not written down. They were taught by one wandering performer to another. The first blues songs were folk songs, often sung by African Americans in the rural South to accompany their labor in the fields. "Southern Negroes sang about everything. Trains, steamboats, steam whistles, sledge hammers, fast women, mean bosses, stubborn mules," Handy wrote. These songs dealt with everyday subjects, but they expressed the contents of aching hearts. They sounded unique to many ears because they employed notes that seemed flat or out of tune when compared to music written by white Americans or Europeans.

In the summer of 1916, Handy hired William Grant Still to arrange songs and play in his band on a performing tour of the South. The tour brought the band to Beale Street, in the Mississippi River port of Memphis, Tennessee. Beale Street was famous for its music, attracting blues musicians from the Mississippi Delta.

The son of slaves, W.C. Handy became one of the most famous African-American musicians of the early 1900s. *(Courtesy of the Library of Congress.)*

Still began attending Oberlin Conservatory in 1917, where his talent was immediately noticed and encouraged by the faculty. *(Courtesy of the Library of Congress.)*

Night after night, fans passed through the swinging doors of saloons such as Pee Wee's and the Hole in the Wall to hear the sounds that they loved.

On Beale Street, Still discovered a distinct beauty in the strong, world-weary voices of blues singers. In the singing and instrumental music alike he heard "a yearning for unattainable happiness," he said. Still explained, "I learned . . . to appreciate the beauty of the blues, and to consider this the musical expression of a lowly people."

His fellow musicians turned out to be kind and decent friends rather than the unsavory characters his mother had predicted they would be. The other band members praised Still's arrangements and encouraged him to write music of his own.

In letters and during Will's occasional visits to Danville, Grace urged him on as well. After his mother sent Will a modest inheritance from his father on his twenty-second birthday, it was Grace's idea that he use the money to study at the Oberlin Conservatory of Music, as he had long dreamed of doing.

Still left Handy's band and in 1917 enrolled at Oberlin, where the teachers quickly spotted his talent. One day, Professor Frederick J. Lehmann had his class set to music "Good-Night," a poem by the African-American writer Paul Laurence Dunbar:

> The lark is silent in his nest,
> The breeze is sighing in its flight,
> Sleep, Love, and peaceful be thy rest,
> Good-night, my love, good-night, good-night.

Lehmann was so impressed by Still's setting of the poem that he advised the young man to pursue composing. Still replied sadly that further study would be impossible. "I told him that I did not have the money," Still said. Although he had been playing music at a nearby theater to accompany silent films, working as a janitor and waiter, and wearing worn-out clothes, his inheritance was just about gone.

Hating to lose such a promising student, Lehmann met with the rest of the faculty to discuss Still's future. He arranged for Will to receive lessons in composition at no cost from another teacher at Oberlin, Dr. George Andrews. Under Dr. Andrews's guidance, Still strived to imitate the styles of the great composers as he wrote music of his own.

Soon world events, and not financial troubles, interrupted Will's musical education. In April 1917, the United States entered World War I. Burning with patriotism like thousands of other young American men, Will left Oberlin to enlist in the armed forces.

In this war, the United States and its allies, including Great Britain, France, and Russia, fought in Europe against the Central Powers: Austria-Hungary, Germany, and Turkey. The Allies battled to secure the independence of small nations in eastern Europe and to end German and Austro-Hungarian aggression.

World War I created divisions among African Americans. Some insisted it was wrong for black soldiers to die protecting the freedom of Europeans as long as they faced discrimination at home. Others said with the world in crisis, African Americans should put aside their hopes for equality and work to win the war. Most notable among the second group was W.E.B. Du Bois. Du Bois called on his fellow black Americans to "forget our special grievances and close our ranks shoulder to shoulder with our white fellow citizens and the allied nations that are fighting for democracy." Despite the divided opinions, more than four hundred thousand African Americans served in World War I, although only forty-two thousand saw combat. The majority performed menial labor, including driving trucks, loading and unloading ships, and serving white officers.

William Grant Still tried to join an army band, but the army already had all of the musicians that it needed. Instead, he enlisted in the navy as a mess attendant, third class. All of the African Americans in the navy

While Still was in the navy, his wife gave birth to one of their four children. *(Courtesy of the University of Arkansas.)*

were restricted to mess detail. They cooked and served meals, washed dishes, and laundered clothes. Will packed a few belongings, including his violin, and went to New York City to await orders.

Great musicians from all over the world performed in New York's concert halls in the early twentieth century, just as they do today. While in New York, Will attended a performance at the famed Metropolitan Opera House. The opera presented that night was Guiseppe Verdi's tragic *Rigoletto,* about a hunchbacked court jester whose daughter becomes the innocent victim of scheming and corruption. Still had listened to operas on records, but never before had he seen one on stage. The majesty of grand opera was unlike anything he had experienced. He vividly recalled the powerful voices, the rich tones of the orchestra, and the glamour of the lush costumes and scenery as he traveled to Norfolk, Virginia. There, he boarded the USS *Kroonland,* the ship to which he had been assigned.

The navy used the *Kroonland* to transport soldiers across the Atlantic Ocean to fight in France. As a mess attendant, Still laundered the white officers' uniforms and waited on the officers at dinner—but not for long. Once word of his musical skill got around, the officers had him play his violin while they dined, and he no longer waited on tables.

It was bad enough that the navy was segregated in 1918, and that African-American sailors were restricted to lowly tasks, but Still learned racism in the armed forces could be even uglier. On one occasion, he witnessed a white army officer whipping black soldiers with a belt, much as the white policeman had beaten a black man in Little Rock years earlier. It was against military regulations for an officer to abuse enlisted men in this way, but none of the whites aboard the ship cared enough to report the incident, and none of the blacks dared to do so.

The mess attendants found ways, however, to look after their own. Once, the *Kroonland* transported one of the army's few African-American officers, who was reporting for duty overseas. Not one of the white officers aboard ship would socialize with this man. In fact, the whites sat as far away from him as they could at meals, crowding into one half of the dining room and leaving him to eat alone in the other half. The mess attendants made sure the black officer received the choicest food and the best service, and through their actions let him know some people appreciated his contribution to the war effort.

World War I was waged at sea as well as on land. On July 10, 1918, as the *Kroonland* was steaming home from France, a lookout spotted the periscope of a German submarine just two hundred yards away. As the crew opened fire, the sky filled with bitter blue smoke. The wounded sub staggered through the water and then sank to the ocean bottom.

The war ended in November 1918. After being discharged that winter, Still labored in a New Jersey shipyard, bailing icy water from the bottoms of ships. After a trip to Danville in January 1919, he was grateful to be hired to play his violin with the Whispering Orchestra, an African-American group in Columbus, Ohio. By spring, he had managed to save some money and returned to Oberlin to resume his studies with Dr. Andrews.

Still was back at Oberlin but feeling restless again. Writing music in the styles of dead composers bored him. The conservatory felt like a cage, and he needed to break out, to plunge into the world of music and discover his own composing style. A few months later, he left Oberlin for the second and final time and headed for New York.

Chapter Four

New York

Manhattan in 1919 was a busy metropolis of five million people. It was a city growing upward, a narrow island covered with pavement and tall buildings. It was a place where people rode elevators or climbed endless flights of stairs to reach apartments and offices. Cars and pedestrians clogged the streets while subway trains rumbled below ground and airplanes crisscrossed the skyline. In 1918, the first regular airmail route had opened, and airplanes transported letters daily between New York and Washington, D.C.

Like William Grant Still, W.C. Handy had come to New York. With lyricist Harry H. Pace, he had formed the Pace and Handy Music Company to publish songs by African Americans. In 1919, Handy hired Still for twenty-five dollars a week to play in his band by night and arrange songs for Pace and Handy by day. Grace Still also moved to New York, bringing her parents and the children. A son, William, had been born in 1916,

Still *(seated at left)* taught himself orchestration while working at Pace and Handy Music Company in New York. *(Courtesy of Duke University.)*

and a daughter, Gail, had been born in 1918. For the first time, Will and his family lived together, and Will got to know his young children. He played with them often because he hated to see them unhappy. When they grew old enough, he joined their outdoor games and taught them to ride bicycles.

The Pace and Handy office was on Broadway, in the heart of New York's theater district, and African-American entertainers were always stopping in to hear the latest songs. Still chatted with such well-known people as tap dancer Bill "Bojangles" Robinson, a popular stage performer, and arranger Will Vodery, whose talents were always in demand on Broadway. He picked the brains of Vodery and other musicians because he was teaching himself orchestration, a difficult skill that composers must learn thoroughly. When orchestrating a work, a composer writes parts for the many different instruments in an orchestra to create a desired sound when they are all played together. Orchestration is similar to arranging, but much more complex.

Still experimented as he learned. He was curious to know what it would sound like if all of the instruments played the same note at once. He also wondered if it was possible to create layers of sound. He thought about music all the time and carried a small notebook in which he jotted down ideas for compositions. He had begun to write short pieces with humorous titles such as "The Tumblebug's Lament" and "The Cross-Eyed Monkey." It is impossible to know how these early works sounded because they have been lost. In later years, as his ability improved, Still was unhappy with his first attempts at composing and threw many of his early pieces away.

Still also did arrangements for Eubie Blake and Noble Sissle, two African Americans who were writing the songs for *Shuffle Along,* a musical show with an all-black cast. *Shuffle Along* opened in New York in the spring of 1921, and immediately became a hit with white audiences. The show introduced a fast-stepping, high-kicking dance called the Charleston, which became one of the biggest fads of the Roaring Twenties.

Still *(seated fourth from right)* arranged music for the production of Eubie Blake's *Shuffle Along*, and later toured with the orchestra. *(Courtesy of the University of Arkansas.)*

After seeing *Shuffle Along,* white America was eager for more black entertainment, and shows with names like *Chocolate Dandies* and *Blackbirds* drew crowds to New York's theaters.

In 1922, when Eubie Blake took a group of actors and musicians on the road to perform *Shuffle Along* in other northeastern cities, William Grant Still went with him as a member of the orchestra. Even on this trip, he kept on learning. While the cast was in Boston, he took lessons in composition from George W. Chadwick, a New England composer known for his operas. Unlike the teachers at Oberlin, Chadwick encouraged Still to write whatever music appealed to his imagination. Chadwick would look over his student's work as he puffed on his pipe, making suggestions that Still was free to accept or reject.

When he returned to New York at the end of the four-month tour, William Grant Still went to work for Black Swan Records. Harry H. Pace had started this company to make recordings of African-American performers. Pace's company filled a real need because most recording companies were owned by whites who refused to have black musicians as clients.

One day, Pace received a letter from the French-born composer Edgard Varèse. Varèse wrote that while crossing the Atlantic on an ocean liner he had met Colonel Charles Young, the highest-ranking African American in the U.S. Army. Varèse was so impressed with Colonel Young that he decided to teach an African-American student at no charge. He asked if Pace knew someone to recommend.

Harry Pace had a lot on his mind. The Black Swan Record Company was not taking in enough money to be profitable, and he was worried about staying in business. He had no time to think about Varèse's request. Will looked on in dismay as Pace held the letter over a wastebasket, and simply had to speak up. "Now wait. Hold it," he cried. "Give that to me. I want that." Will got Pace's recommendation and the chance to study with Varèse.

Edgard Varèse, who had moved to the United States in 1915, was devoted to taking music in new directions. In the early twentieth century, he and other modern composers were trying to create music that most people

The Charleston, a dance that was choreographed for the all-black musical *Shuffle Along*, swept the nation during the Roaring Twenties. *(Courtesy of the Library of Congress.)*

would not have considered musical. Varèse wrote music that was strongly dissonant, or deliberately harsh. Instead of the pleasing harmonies, or blends of notes, that composers traditionally had used, Varèse called for clashing notes to be played together. (One way to hear such dissonance is to play any two keys that are next to each other on a piano keyboard at the same time.) Varèse also avoided recognizable melodies and pat-

terns, which for centuries had helped listeners under-
stand musical works.

Like George Chadwick, Varèse wanted Will to develop his own musical ideas—but only up to a point. If
Will wrote anything melodic or reminiscent of the past,
Varèse gave him a stern warning: "Don't get soft!" As a
result, much of the music Still wrote during his two
years of study with Varèse, from 1923 until 1925, was
dissonant. One such piece was *From the Land of Dreams,*
composed for three female voices with instrumental
accompaniment. The women were to sing without words,
as if their voices were three more musical instruments.
In this work, Still tried to convey the fleeting nature of
dreams, which are so vivid during sleep but dissolve
upon waking.

On February 8, 1925, *From the Land of Dreams* was
performed in a concert organized by the International
Composers' Guild, a group founded in 1921 to show-
case modern music. As Still shared his work with a
listening audience for the first time, he felt as though
he had exposed his most private thoughts and feelings.
"I was so nervous when it was being played that I
scarcely heard it," he admitted.

The concert over, he waited impatiently to read what
music critics would write about his work in New York
City's newspapers. Good reviews would interest many
people in his music and build his reputation, but bad
reviews might make it hard to have his compositions
performed in the future.

Some critics found things to like about *From the*

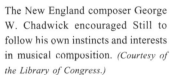

The New England composer George W. Chadwick encouraged Still to follow his own instincts and interests in musical composition. *(Courtesy of the Library of Congress.)*

Land of Dreams. One remarked, "Mr. Still has a very sensuous approach to music." Others, though, wrote negative reviews. Olin Downes, the influential music critic for the *New York Times,* called Still's piece "an incoherent fantasy." Downes also implied African Americans should stay out of the concert hall and limit themselves to writing simple, catchy songs. Still would do better to compose "the rollicking and often original and entertaining music performed in Negro [musicals]," he commented. Those words hurt. *From the Land of Dreams* was never played again, and for the rest of his life, Still claimed he had discarded it.

Still did say this, however: "It is not Still but Varèse who speaks in *From the Land of Dreams.*" In other words, he had been trying too hard to write music that sounded like his teacher's discordant works; it was time to develop his own style. Still began to look for ideas in African-American history and culture. He had no wish to write the "rollicking" songs that people like Olin Downes expected from a black composer; instead, he hoped to create serious music based on African-American themes. In taking this turn, Still was influenced by the writers and artists of the Harlem Renaissance.

In the years after World War I, black poets, novelists, painters, and sculptors had formed an artistic community in Harlem, in northern Manhattan. In a flowering of creativity known as the Harlem Renaissance, they celebrated African-American life. Harlem Renaissance poets such as Claude McKay and Langston Hughes wrote about their people's hopes and sorrows, while painters such as Aaron Douglas created bold works inspired by African art. Black America was "finding a new soul," wrote Professor Alain Locke of Howard University in Washington, D.C., who helped to popularize the Harlem Renaissance in the 1920s. "There is a renewed race-spirit that consciously and proudly sets itself apart."

The music of Harlem nights was a new form called jazz, which was hot, ever-changing, and alive. A jazz performance was like a conversation, as musicians played with rhythms and melodies and bounced riffs, or musical phrases, off one another.

Still's next piece of music combined the stirring sounds of jazz, the bent notes of the blues, and the sometimes jarring chords of modern music. *Levee Land* was a set of four short works for a soprano and a small orchestra. Once again, Still used the human voice as an instrument, having the vocalist sing simple words, such as "hey," and "baby." The singer was to give the words meaning by the way she sang, making them express sorrow, playfulness, or surprise.

Levee Land was first performed in New York's Aeolian Hall on January 24, 1926, and featured Florence Mills, one of the most popular entertainers of the 1920s. Nicknamed the "Queen of Happiness," Mills was known for her vibrant personality and clear, delicate voice. Still had met her in 1925, when he was playing in the orchestra of *From Dixie to Broadway,* an all-black musical in which Florence Mills starred.

This time, there was no doubt that the audience loved what they heard. The crowd applauded so loudly and

Will played many instruments, including the cello. *(Courtesy of the University of Arkansas.)*

Still lived and worked in New York City during the Roaring Twenties.
(Courtesy of the Library of Congress.)

for so long that Florence Mills and the musicians re-
peated the performance, from start to finish. *Levee Land*
puzzled some reviewers, though. For example, one per-
plexed critic suggested Still had applied Albert Einstein's
theories of relativity to his music. In the early twentieth
century, Einstein published theories that changed the
way physicists viewed time, space, and gravity. Einstein's
ideas confused much of the general public, and the
reviewer found Still's music to be just as perplexing.
Most reviewers, however, agreed with the critic who

wrote, "These works are so good, healthy, sane . . . that they place this Negro composer on a high plane."

Despite such praise, Still credited Florence Mills with *Levee Land*'s success. Mills died suddenly of a burst appendix in 1927, and from then on, Still turned down any offers to have *Levee Land* performed again. "Where can we find another Florence Mills?" he asked.

Still kept on writing and completed *Darker America,* an orchestral piece in which different instruments tell the story of blacks in the United States. The composer explained *Darker America* was "intended to suggest the triumph of a people over their sorrows through fervent prayer." In this work, string instruments play a theme representing the African-American people, while the English horn suggests sorrow. Sorrow alternates with another theme, hope, which features muted brass instruments. For a time, "the people seem about to rise above their troubles. But sorrow triumphs," Still noted. At last, a prayer is offered, played on an oboe. At the conclusion of *Darker America,* Still seems to look into the future, foreseeing a time when, with God's help, his people would overcome racial injustice.

In 1926, Still found a friend in Howard Hanson, director of the Eastman School of Music in Rochester, New York. Hanson selected *Darker America* to be performed in a concert at the school. Hanson, too, was a composer, and he was dedicated to bringing American music to the public's attention. He liked to present old and new musical works together in concert, thus "enabling the hearers to form some estimate of the direction in which American music is moving," he said.

Not only did the Eastman School of Music award Still a prize for *Darker America,* Hanson recommended Still's music to conductors and teachers. He also hired Still to lecture on composition to students at the school. At age thirty, tall, sandy-haired Howard Hanson was just a year younger than William Grant Still. The two men would remain friends for life.

Will was gratified all of his hard work was finally paying off, but he was especially pleased that his mother knew of his success. Carrie Shepperson had cancer and was too ill to travel to New York to hear her son's music performed, but she read newspaper accounts of his concerts and let him know she was proud. Carrie Shepperson died in 1927; she did not live long enough to see her son win an award from the Harmon Foundation, which honored African Americans for outstanding work in the arts, in 1928.

In 1928, Still also began to write *Africa*, a work for the orchestra that was a fanciful portrait of the African homeland. He titled its three parts, or movements, "Land of Peace," "Land of Romance," and "Land of Superstition." It seemed to Still that African Americans viewed the continent of their forbears as a place of serene landscapes and untroubled minds. Africa was the source of myths and folktales that lived on among the African Americans of the South. It was also a land of pagan beliefs, where spirits were thought to live in nature and people practiced witchcraft.

So much was happening, and so fast. In 1929, Still

traveled to Los Angeles to arrange songs for a radio program devoted to jazz. Jobs such as this one took time away from composing, but they helped him support his large family. Two more children, June and Caroline, had been born in 1920 and 1925. Still refused to be discouraged by the popular music that he was paid to arrange and play, telling himself, "I'm going to use it. I'm going to let it teach me something." And teach him it did. Throughout his career as a composer, he would include the sounds of jazz and the blues—popular American musical forms—in the ballets, operas, and symphonies that he wrote.

Los Angeles was a city vastly different from New York. Instead of growing up, Los Angeles had spread out, covering more than 440 square miles. Its streets led west to the Pacific Ocean, north to the San Gabriel Mountains, and east to orange groves. William Grant Still knew he could be happy living and working in warm, friendly California.

When the radio job ended in 1930, Still returned to New York City with his mind full of ideas for compositions. Many nights he ate dinner with a friend, the African-American playwright Carlton Moss, at the Harlem YMCA. Moss recalled, Still "would sit there, and he had this habit of tapping his foot. He never talked about anything else but that music . . . I got the impression that when he left me, wherever he went, he'd sit down and mess with that music." It appeared to Moss that Still "was always off, in another world."

William Grant Still would have agreed. He once said, "Music is just every bit of me."

Chapter Five

"With Humble Thanks"

In 1927, Alain Locke, the Howard University professor, sent Still a story called "Sahdji," by a writer named Richard Bruce, which was set in Central Africa in an earlier time. Locke suggested Still compose music for a ballet based on this tale of a chieftain's unfaithful wife. "Frankly, I would like to see you try your hand at this," Locke wrote. "Will you? Does it interest you?"

Still read about the beautiful Sahdji, favorite wife of the chieftain Konombju, and how she falls in love with her husband's nephew, Mrabo. When Chief Konombju is killed on a hunting trip, Sahdji faces a difficult decision: Should she conform to the tribal custom and take her own life, or should she seek happiness with her new love? As Sahdji wrestles with her heart, she dances before her husband's bier. Finally, the choice made, she lifts a sacrificial dagger and plunges it into her body.

Even as he read, Still heard melodies in his mind. Soon, he was learning everything he could about the music of Africa, music in which drumbeats abounded. African musicians created complex rhythms. It was not uncommon for drummers to play two or three rhythms at once, or for people to add to the rhythmic mix by clapping their hands or stamping their feet. Africans traditionally sang throughout the day, creating songs to mark marriages, births, and deaths, or to call the villagers to hunt or to war.

Hoping through music to transport his audience to Africa, Still composed a ballet that pulsed with drums, from its rumbling beginning to the sudden thunderclap of its conclusion. A chorus played the role of African villagers, setting the scene through song:

> In the heart of the jungle,
> In the middle of the forest,
> In the center of the hearth-fire.

The clapping of the chorus added another layer of rhythm as a male singer stood apart, chanting African proverbs that commented on the action of the ballet. "Death is at the end of the rope," he recited, foreshadowing Sahdji's tragic end. As Sahdji and her lover, Mrabo, entered a hut, the singer chanted, "The fig tree does not call the birds," implying that Sahdji was responsible for her own actions.

Still dedicated *Sahdji* to his friend Howard Hanson. On May 22, 1931, *Sahdji* became the first ballet to be featured in Hanson's American music concerts at the Eastman School of Music.

Still suspected *Sahdji* would be well received when he learned from Howard Hanson that after playing the music at a rehearsal, the orchestra members had put down their instruments to applaud. "As you know," Hanson said, "this is most unusual for a professional group and it only shows how deeply impressed they were with your music." Still knew he had succeeded on the night of the performance when the audience responded to his ballet with enthusiasm. The critics all had good things to say about *Sahdji,* and even Olin Downes of the *New York Times* saw beyond Still's race and praised him as one of America's finest composers. Downes wrote, "This is real music, music of a composer of exotic talent and temperament, who has a keen sense of beauty."

Hanson had loaned Still the money he needed to travel to Rochester for the event because the composer could not afford to pay for the trip himself. Like millions of Americans, William Grant Still was feeling the impact of the Great Depression, a prolonged period of economic hardship that had begun in 1929. Across the nation, men and women lost their jobs as factories and other businesses closed. Black workers were often the first to be fired, and by 1931, unemployment among blacks in many cities was thirty to sixty percent higher than it was among whites. People had less money to spend on entertainment, so musicians also saw their incomes decline or disappear.

Will was also dealing with discord at home. As he struggled to pay the bills, Grace Still secretly withdrew money from the bank and spent it on herself. The couple argued, and Will strived to hold his temper. He relied on his faith, writing in his diary, "I believe that God will clear away my trouble."

At least being out of work gave Still time to compose music. For a long time, he had wanted to write a symphony that elevated the blues, or wove elements of this African-American musical style into a major work for the orchestra. "It was not until the depression struck that I went jobless long enough to let the Symphony take shape," he said. "In 1930, I rented a room in a quiet building not far from my home in New York, and began to work." The result of Still's effort was the *Afro-American Symphony,* his most famous piece, which was inspired by the experiences of African Americans after the Civil War.

On October 30, 1930, Still noted in his diary that he had begun the difficult task of composing the symphony. "Things look dark. I pray for the strength that I may do just as God would have me," he wrote.

The symphony took shape over the next several weeks. Sometimes musical ideas came to Still while he was sleeping. He began each workday by writing down the fragments of melody and harmony that he remembered from his dreams. On November 5, he jotted in his diary, "I received some splendid ideas for the Afro-American Symphony last night." At last, the symphony was finished, and Still marked it with the words that he wrote on all his completed works: "With humble thanks to God, The source of all inspiration."

The four movements of the *Afro-American Symphony* express emotions that Still attributed to the African Americans of an earlier era, the years after the Civil War, beginning with a longing for their homeland. The first movement, which opens and closes with the sound of the blues, conveys the yearning in the heart of a lonely people. The second movement gives voice to sorrow, as the sounds of horns and string instruments intertwine in a melody reminiscent of a spiritual.

The third movement is Still's interpretation of African Americans' humor. It is a great "Hallelujah!" consisting of uplifting music punctuated by clashing cymbals. The entire orchestra plays a lively theme that is echoed by different instruments in turn—horns, violins, and flutes. In this way, Still represents in music the many personal stories that make up the saga of the African-American people. The beautiful fourth movement of the *Afro-American Symphony* blends memories of past sorrows with hope to portray nobility.

The first performance of Still's symphony, which took place in Rochester on October 28, 1931, brought the audience to its feet. All of the critics wrote glowing reviews, including the writer for the *Rochester Evening Journal,* who stated: "The symphony has life and sparkle when needed and a deep haunting beauty . . . It laughs unrestrainedly, it mourns dolefully."

Once again, Howard Hanson had sent Still the money to make the trip, but bad weather had forced the composer's flight to be cancelled, and he had to wait until the second performance at the Eastman School, on

March 31, 1932, to hear his symphony played by an orchestra. Praising Hanson, Still asked, "Do you see now why I admire him so much when, in addition to encouraging me as he does, he offers me material aid of that sort?"

The Stills' financial problems had begun to ease in late 1931, when Will was hired to arrange songs for Willard Robison's "Deep River Hour," a popular program on WOR radio in New York. Robison was a singer who in the 1920s formed the Deep River Orchestra. On their radio program, which despite its name was a half hour long, Robison and his band entertained listeners with their versions of popular songs.

For one hundred dollars a week, Still created arrangements for the orchestra when it accompanied Robison's singing, as well as purely instrumental arrangements for the musicians alone. He wanted listeners to come away from the program feeling uplifted, and he believed he succeeded. He called his arrangements for the radio show "the best I ever made."

Many of Still's arrangements are in collections at the Smithsonian Institution and elsewhere, but many others have been lost. In 1948, Sigmund Spaeth, a well-known music historian, commented, "It is impossible to estimate the extent of his contributions to the lighter music of America."

Willard Robison also asked Still to conduct the all-white orchestra during broadcasts, making him the first black conductor to lead a white orchestra in New York. One musician, who was from the South, refused to play

Radio served as a major source of entertainment for Americans during the Great Depression. *(Courtesy of the Library of Congress.)*

under an African-American conductor and left the group. He soon had a change of heart, however, and asked to rejoin the orchestra. Not only did Still forgive the man, but he became his friend as well. In 1933, when the program moved to NBC radio, station executives refused to let an African American lead the orchestra, and a white conductor took over.

The steady job failed to ease the tension in the Still household, though. Will now gave Grace sixty dollars a week and additional money for food, but it was not enough to keep the family together. In September 1932, Grace took the children and moved to Canada, telling Will she planned to work for a magazine, and leaving him with only the family dog, Shep, for company.

William Grant Still had relied on his dreams for inspiration. Now he studied them for messages of hope. In February 1933, he described one of his dreams in a letter to a friend and explained what it meant to him:

> I stood in the rear of a large concert hall where a symphony orchestra was rehearsing. My attention was centered on the orchestra until it was suddenly directed to one of the seats in the rear of the hall. On it I saw the score of AFRICA bound in a handsome red cover on which the title had been stamped in letters of gold. I am sure this was a prophetic vision. The red cover was a symbol of happiness and the gold letters a symbol of success.

As Still's music began to be heard overseas, the prophecy seemed to be coming true. Howard Hanson conducted the Berlin Philharmonic Orchestra in a performance of the third movement of the *Afro-American Symphony* in January 1933. The German audience liked Still's piece so much that they called for the musicians to play it again—and then again. Also in 1933, *Africa* was included in a concert in Paris.

Still also took pride in another composition. *La Guiablesse* was a ballet based on a legend from the Caribbean island of Martinique. La Guiablesse was a devil who was able to disguise herself as a beautiful woman. In the story she lures a young man away from his true love and to his death.

Katherine Dunham received glowing reviews for her dancing in *La Guiablesse*. *(Courtesy of the Library of Congress.)*

Once again, in 1933, a work by William Grant Still had its first performance at the Eastman School in Rochester, and again the critics had good things to say. Wrote one, "The music is charming, picturesque, and dramatically suggestive." *La Guiablesse* was also performed in 1934 in Chicago, with a young dancer named Katherine Dunham in her first leading role. Dunham would go on to become one of the most important African-American dancers of the twentieth century.

Still had composed two ballets, a symphony, and a variety of shorter works, but he had yet to fulfill his dream of writing an opera. In 1934, he applied for funds from the Guggenheim Foundation, an organization that supports people working in a variety of fields, including the creative arts. If he won a Guggenheim Fellowship, Still planned to use the money to support himself while writing an opera. Also, as he wrote in his application, "I should like to go to California . . . for there I find an atmosphere conducive to creative effort."

Luck was on Still's side. He received the fellowship and resigned from his job with the "Deep River Hour." On May 22, 1934, he loaded Shep and a few belongings into a car and started out for Los Angeles. "California did something to me," he said in an interview in 1967. "And I can't tell you what it was . . . When I came here, it was like coming home."

Chapter Six

Billy

William Grant Still had waited so long to write an opera that once he began, the music rushed from his mind. He wrote day and night, and in a short time he completed *Blue Steel*. Based on a story by Carlton Moss, his friend in New York, Still's first opera told a tale of Vodou, a religion that blends African rituals and beliefs with elements of Roman Catholicism. Vodou originated in the Caribbean nation of Haiti but has followers in the southern United States as well.

A new West Coast friend, Harold Bruce Forsythe, wrote the libretto, or lyrics, for *Blue Steel*. Forsythe was a writer and musician who had been inspired by the Harlem Renaissance to promote the work of African-American artists in the western states. Another new friend, Verna Arvey, served as Still's secretary and musical assistant. The daughter of Jewish immigrants from Russia, Arvey was a journalist and pianist who performed in the Los Angeles area and on the radio. She was a thoughtful, studious young woman who loved beautiful music. In the relaxed atmosphere of California, Still became known to his new friends as Billy.

Some of those friends were singers, and on a night soon after Still finished the opera, they came to his house and sang the roles. The weather was warm, and neighbors lingered outside to hear the music pouring from Still's open windows. They heard melodies reminding them now of jazz and now of spirituals, sung by rich, polished voices. When the opera ended and the singers fell silent, applause came from porches up and down the street.

Still's Los Angeles neighbors may have loved *Blue Steel,* but not a single opera company in the United States would agree to perform it. Too many people were blinded by prejudice, refusing to believe an African American could write an opera. A disappointed Still put *Blue Steel* away, but he kept on learning and composing. "There are no shortcuts or detours," he said.

> Quick, glittering successes are hardly worth taking. In the beginning I looked with despair on the work of the masters. I didn't even know how to work out my own little ideas. But miraculously . . . there came the opportunity to learn, and though often I didn't have enough to eat, the stubbornness in me kept me going. Somehow, I never lost faith.

On July 23, 1936, Still made musical history when he conducted the Los Angeles Philharmonic Orchestra

Verna Arvey worked as Still's musical assistant and later became his wife.
(Courtesy of the University of Arkansas.)

at the Hollywood Bowl. Although a hundred conductors from fifteen different countries had led concerts in the outdoor amphitheater, every one had been white. For the first time in the United States, an African American led a major orchestra. Still conducted a concert of American music that included "Land of Romance" from the orchestral work *Africa,* and the lively third movement of the *Afro-American Symphony.*

In 1936, Still also worked for Columbia Pictures, a Hollywood movie studio, writing and arranging music for motion-picture soundtracks. Many songwriters were earning high salaries composing music for films, and with four faraway children needing his support, Still looked forward to receiving a good income. He wrote music for *Theodora Goes Wild,* a comedy film about a small-town woman who writes a bestselling book, and *Pennies from Heaven,* a musical starring the popular singer Bing Crosby.

Despite his achievements in Hollywood, Still was unhappy. In his opinion, the movie studio was like an enormous factory, and his employers seemed not to recognize his talent and ability. They also misunderstood his sense of humor. One day, as a joke, Still penciled in notes for a loud trumpet solo while he was writing the background music for a quiet movie scene. He intended to erase the solo before the musicians began to play but never got the chance. Suddenly, a trumpet blared during the rehearsal, startling everyone in the room. The bosses found nothing amusing about Still's prank, and they fired him.

A composer of William Grant Still's stature belonged in the world of serious music and not in the movie business. By 1937, he was hard at work on *Troubled Island,* an opera based on the life of Jean Jacques Dessalines. Dessalines had been born into slavery, but he served as the first ruler of the newly independent nation of Haiti from 1804 until his assassination in 1806.

The Harlem Renaissance poet Langston Hughes came to California to work with Still on the libretto for this new opera. Cautioning Hughes, Still said, "Please remember that it is absolutely necessary for us to keep in touch if we are to collaborate." Despite Still's request, Hughes took off for Spain when his work was done, to report for a Baltimore newspaper on the civil war that was being fought in that European country.

As Still wrote the music for *Troubled Island,* he discovered the libretto needed some changes. Here and

Langston Hughes, a writer of the Harlem Renaissance, collaborated on the libretto of *Troubled Island. (Courtesy of the Library of Congress.)*

there, the lyrics had to be altered to sound more melodious or to fit the music that he had composed. With Langston Hughes far away, Still asked for Verna Arvey's help. She proved to be a talented librettist, and the two made a good creative team.

Still submitted *Troubled Island* to opera companies across the nation, hoping to find one willing to perform it. As he waited for a response, he and Verna Arvey collaborated on *Lenox Avenue,* a suite, or set of related pieces, inspired by the sights and sounds of a famous Harlem thoroughfare. *Lenox Avenue* was written for an orchestra and chorus with an announcer whose words guided listeners from one episode to the next. After it was broadcast to the nation over the CBS radio network on May 23, 1937, more than one hundred listeners sent letters of praise to the radio station. "I have a difficult time enjoying or understanding most of the modern compositions of our day, but this music impressed me differently," one person wrote. "From the depth and warmth of the music emerged a soul."

Such comments told Still that he was on the right path. He had come to believe modern composers who wrote discordant music had lost touch with their audience. He had been striving instead to compose music that came from the heart, with melodies and rhythms that listeners could recognize and enjoy. He said, "Just as the spark of freedom burns in the hearts of people all over the world, whether they be free men or oppressed, so does the inner love of beauty, and so does the public appreciation of all that is worthy in the arts."

Still hoped the public would also love his next piece for the concert hall, the *Symphony in G Minor.* While the *Afro-American Symphony* had been inspired by the African Americans of the past, the new symphony celebrated Still's contemporaries, black Americans living in the first half of the twentieth century. "It may be said that the purpose of the Symphony in G Minor is to point musically to changes wrought in a people through the progressive and transmuting spirit of America," the composer explained.

Since the time of the First World War, thousands of African Americans had moved from the rural South to the industrial centers of the North. In a population shift known as the Great Migration, people went north to find steady jobs in factories and good schools for their children, and to escape racial discrimination. Trains had carried as many as 1.4 million people to Chicago, New York, and other northern cities between 1916 and 1928.

Still's second symphony began with a flutter of sound that was as gentle as a bird in flight. Then, like a locomotive, the music quickly gained speed and volume until it became a driving force accented by trumpets and drums. Listeners knew immediately this symphony pointed confidently toward the future. Because hope thrived in the hearts of individuals, Still portrayed this personal optimism in the quiet sections of the symphony, especially in the thoughtful, melodious second movement, which featured the sounds of string instruments.

Although Still viewed the African Americans of his day as people taking control of their destiny, most had faced obstacles upon reaching the North. The majority were forced to take low-paying jobs that offered no chance of advancement. Landlords charged the newcomers high rents for rundown housing in poor neighborhoods. And not only did children attend schools that were segregated by custom rather than by law, but city life exposed young people to alcohol and drug use and crime.

The Philadelphia Orchestra, conducted by Leopold Stokowski, introduced the *Symphony in G Minor* to the world in December 1937. Stokowski, who greatly admired the piece, called it the "Song of a New Race," giving it a name that people continue to use today.

As Still completed his symphony, a committee in New York was searching for a composer to write the theme music for a great world's fair that was to open in their city in 1939. The committee members listened to recordings of many pieces of music and liked two the best: *Lenox Avenue* and a suite called *A Deserted Plantation*. The composer of either piece, they said, deserved the job. The planners of the 1939 New York World's Fair were surprised to learn that both pieces had been written by the same person, William Grant Still. They commissioned Still to write the fair's theme music and invited him to New York to see the plans for the Persiphere. This steel and concrete ball, two hundred feet in diameter, was to symbolize the fair's motto, "Building the World of Tomorrow."

When the World's Fair opened on April 30, 1939, the United States had yet to recover fully from the Great Depression. In Europe, Adolph Hitler's Nazi troops had marched out of Germany to occupy Austria and portions of Czechoslovakia. Despite the gloomy news at home and abroad, President Franklin Delano Roosevelt said in his opening-day address, "Our wagon is hitched to a star . . . a star of good will, a star of progress for mankind, a star of greater happiness and less hardship, a star of international good will, and, above all, a star of peace."

Visitors to the fair wanted to forget the world's troubles. Upon entering the Persiphere, they stepped onto revolving balconies to view Democracity, a model of an imagined city of the year 2039. During the six minutes that it took for the balconies to revolve once around the model, fairgoers heard a recording of Still's theme music performed by an orchestra and chorus. A writer for the *New Yorker* magazine estimated that during the summers of 1939 and 1940, when the fair was open, Still's theme was played 31,857 times.

Still had always hoped his music would help to break racial barriers, and now for the first time, an African American had been selected to write an important piece of music without regard for his race. He said, "I must admit that I can't help but be proud of the distinction."

He shared his joy with Verna Arvey. Through years of working together, Billy and Verna had become close friends. Although one was black and the other white, they had gradually fallen in love. "As for myself, I had

Still (*left*) and W.C. Handy in front of the partially completed Persiphere at the 1939 World's Fair in New York City. *(Courtesy of the University of Arkansas.)*

long forgotten any ideas about racial differences—if indeed, I had ever had any in the first place," Arvey said. Others were less accepting of interracial romance, however, and the couple received hate mail. Arvey told Langston Hughes, "We have had a barrage of the dirtiest, lousiest, most malicious anonymous letters you can imagine."

Their love, and not the threats or public disapproval, mattered most to Billy and Verna. Billy obtained a divorce from Grace, and on February 8, 1939, he and Verna drove to Mexico to be married because marriages between blacks and whites were illegal at the time in California. Billy was forty-three years old when he and Verna married, and she was twenty-nine.

Verna and Billy said they "didn't marry because we wanted to prove anything, to make any scientific experiments, or to be smart. We married because, after five years of working together . . . we suddenly realized that we were only happy together, that together we wanted to build a home and to have children." The Stills believed, "If a marriage succeeds, it succeeds not because of racial considerations or in spite of them, but because two individuals are suited to each other."

Chapter Seven

Family Man

Billy and Verna settled in a small stucco house on Cimarron Street in Los Angeles and began a contented life together. Their son, Duncan, was born in 1940, and their daughter, Judith Anne, was born in 1942. Billy was a devoted father to these two children, singing to them when they were babies and reading to them as soon as they were old enough to enjoy books. The man who had made toy violins as a child now built wooden doll furniture and locomotives for Judith and Duncan. Using a fine-bladed coping saw, he cut squares of wood into puzzles.

He continued to support the four children from his first marriage, although he saw them rarely. "Gee, but I love those kids," he confessed to Harold Bruce Forsythe. "I never fully [knew] how greatly I was wrapped up in them until I was separated from them."

There was never money to spare, but in the Still household happiness did not depend on a high income.

Verna said, "As long as we had a roof over our heads, we felt the luxuries could wait."

Like many people with a happy home life, Billy found pleasure in his daily routine. After breakfast with Verna and the children, he went to his workroom. There, wearing a terrycloth robe over his clothes, he sat quietly, summoning the music that had come to him the night before in dreams. He spent the morning sounding out melodies and harmonies on a piano, but in his mind he heard all of the instruments in an orchestra. "The sounds of slowly evolving chords and harmonies coming from the workroom piano were as familiar to us as the smells of the evening honeysuckle or of the sheets fresh from the clothesline," Judith Anne Still remembered. Her father was ready to put notes on paper by noon, and he wrote steadily until 3:30, when he ate a late lunch.

The final hours of the afternoon were the time for tending his vegetable garden or building toys and furniture in the garage. He often could be heard whistling while he worked. At dusk, he listened while Verna played through the day's new music on the piano.

The 1940s were a productive decade in William Grant Still's career. "Those were very happy years for me," he said. "I felt I was actually getting somewhere with my composing." In 1940, he wrote *And They Lynched Him on a Tree*, setting a poem by Katherine Garrison Chapin to music. Chapin had written the poem to persuade Congress to pass a bill that would make lynching a federal crime. Supporters of the proposed law pointed

Still, Verna, and their two children, Duncan and Judith Anne, at the piano in 1944.
(Courtesy of the University of Arkansas.)

out the Southern states were doing almost nothing to stop the lynching of blacks. In fact, 130 lynchings had occurred in the United States in the 1930s, and almost all of the victims had been African American.

Still employed two choruses in this piece, one white and one black, representing the white and black populations of a small southern town. The choruses told a disturbing story of racial hatred and murder.

The piece opens on a dark, cold night as a lynching has just been committed. The white chorus sings, "We've swung him higher than the tallest pine. / We've cut his throat so he ain't goin' ter whine." As the whites leave for home, sounds of engines starting and car horns punctuate the music. Next, there is quiet moaning to indicate the black citizens, now safe, are coming out of hiding. Seeing the murdered man's body, the people sing, "Oh my God, have mercy on me!"

A soloist portraying the victim's mother remembers the day he was born. "Oh sorrow, oh sorrow, you've taken my hand," she laments. "Oh sorrow, I must walk with you to de promised land!" As the gathered people cut down the body, they sing again and again, "He was a man."

And They Lynched Him on a Tree was first performed at Lewisohn Stadium in New York City on June 25, 1940. Billy and Verna listened to the concert on the radio at home because they could not afford to travel across the country to New York. It thrilled them to hear the audience's warm applause and to hear the radio announcer say, "It is not given to many people to witness such a beautiful performance of such a beautiful work."

In 1941, Still set to music another poem by Katherine Garrison Chapin, *Plain Chant for America*. After its first performance in New York, on October 23, 1941, *Plain Chant for America* was played at the Royal Albert Hall in London for British Prime Minister Winston Churchill and the U.S. ambassador. Great Britain was then at war. On September 3, 1939, following Hitler's invasion of Poland, the British and the French had declared war on Germany. Still's music served as a sign of friendship between the British and American people.

Written for a man's voice, orchestra, and organ, this musical work called to mind the trouble in Europe, where "a hemisphere darkens and the nations flame." It also paid tribute to the freedom that Americans enjoy. "No dark signs close the doors of our speaking . . . No bayonets bar the door to our pray'rs, / No gun butts shadow our children's eyes."

The United States entered the war following the surprise attack on the American naval base at Pearl Harbor, Hawaii, on December 7, 1941. In two short hours, Japanese planes had struck and sunk four U.S. battleships and crippled four more. The attackers had destroyed 188 planes belonging to the U.S. fleet and killed 2,403 people. On December 8, President Franklin Delano Roosevelt asked Congress to declare war on Japan, and three days later, Germany and Italy declared war on the United States.

Messman First Class Dorie Miller was one of the first American heroes of the war. This African-American sailor had been on the deck of the battleship *West Virginia* when it was hit by a bomb during the raid on Pearl Harbor. After carrying the ship's wounded captain to safety, he took hold of one of the machine guns that was attached to the ship's deck. He aimed toward the sky and fired, shooting down at least four enemy planes before running out of ammunition. His actions earned him the Navy Cross, the navy's highest decoration for bravery.

Dorie Miller was one of approximately one million African Americans who served in the armed forces during World War II. On Thanksgiving Day 1943, he was stationed aboard an aircraft carrier, the USS *Liscombe Bay,* in the South Pacific, when a Japanese torpedo tore open the ship and sank it. He was among more than six hundred crew members who died.

African Americans had given their lives for liberty since 1770, when British soldiers shot to death a sea-

Congress declared war against Japan on December 8, 1941.
(Courtesy of the Naval Historical Foundation.)

man named Crispus Attucks who had led a protest against their presence in Boston. From that time forward, in every American war, African Americans had fought and died defending freedom that was often denied to them because of their race. In 1943, when the League of Composers invited William Grant Still to write a short, patriotic piece for the radio, he honored these brave men and women. "Our civilization has known no greater patriotism, no greater loyalty than that shown by the colored men who fight and die for democracy," he said. He hoped those who returned from the war would "come back to a better world."

He wrote a four-minute requiem—a work commemorating the dead—called *In Memoriam: The Colored Soldiers Who Died for Democracy.* Critics commenting on the piece said Still had written it "with sympathy and feeling," and the music "says what it has to say directly and tellingly."

During World War II, African Americans made important gains in the military. In 1943, for example, the navy commissioned its first African-American active-duty officers, a group of men known as the "Golden Thirteen." In April of that year, the first squadron of African-American military pilots went overseas. This unit, the 99th Pursuit Squadron, was an experiment for the army because racial prejudice had such a strong hold in the United States that many whites doubted the ability of blacks to fly planes.

Known as the Tuskegee Airmen because they trained to fly fighter planes at an army air base near Tuskegee, Alabama, the men of the 99th supported the invasion of Italy by forces of the United States, Great Britain, and Canada. The Tuskegee Airmen helped to capture Pantelleria, a strategic island off the coast of North Africa, and provided cover from the air as the United States and its allies thrust at the southern Italian island of Sicily on September 10, 1943.

Filled with pride for the black pilots, Still composed a *Fanfare for the 99th Fighter Squadron.* Music lovers first heart this short, dramatic work for horns at the Hollywood Bowl on July 22, 1945.

At the time of the concert, the war in Europe was

over. Germany's unconditional surrender had taken effect on May 8, 1945. Less than a month after the performance, on August 14, Japan surrendered as well. Atomic bombs exploded by the Americans over the Japanese cities of Hiroshima and Nagasaki on August 6 and August 9 had convinced Japan's military to lay down its arms.

After more than four years of war, Americans turned their attention to peaceful pursuits. They enjoyed economic prosperity and focused on their families. Billy and Verna took their children to parks, movies, and museums. Duncan loved to watch trains and ships, so the Stills made many trips to railroad yards and to the Los Angeles waterfront. Recalling her father at this time, Judith Anne Still wrote: "When he was not writing music or reading he was childlike in his pleasures, sometimes reciting nonsense rhymes when he was in a good mood, or reading license plates aloud when he was driving, rolling the sounds of the letters around his tongue. If someone told an especially good joke he laughed until the tears came to his eyes."

William Grant Still had longed for years to see one of his operas performed. It therefore gladdened his heart when he learned, in 1948, that *Troubled Island,* his opera set in Haiti, was going to be presented at the New York City Center for Music and Drama. He wrote to his conductor friend Leopold Stokowski, "This opera is the dream of my life."

Librettist Langston Hughes, who was in New York, attended rehearsals of the opera and described them in letters to the composer. "The City Center is humming with preparations for *Troubled Island,*" he noted. Still's music, he said, "sounds very lovely indeed. It has a lot of melody and so should prove to be a popular opera with the public."

Excitedly, Still traveled to New York to attend the March 31, 1949, debut of his opera. On that night, for the first time, a major American company performed an opera by a black composer. The audience saw scenes in which the runaway slave Jean Jacques Dessalines served as a general in the revolutionary army that freed Haiti from French rule. They saw him crowned emperor of Haiti in 1804, and then watched as he turned into a tyrant who made enemies among his followers. During the final act, after Dessalines has been assassinated, they heard his wife sing a beautiful aria to mourn him.

When the last lyrics had been sung and the final notes from the orchestra had died away, the audience was on its feet, filling the concert hall with deafening applause. Twenty times, the grateful composer walked to center stage to take a bow. It was a magical night for William Grant Still.

Yet to seven-year-old Judith Anne, the man who came home from New York seemed shattered. As an adult, she wrote, "I remember how he looked in his long charcoal grey overcoat and brown, wide-brimmed hat, wearily taking his suitcases out of our '36 Ford after we had brought him home from the airport." He handed small presents to the children, took a small notepad from his pocket, and began to page through it. "Well, Verna," he said to his wife, "I just don't know what to say."

Chapter Eight

"Music is Beauty"

What had happened to turn William Grant Still's triumph into defeat? He told his wife that while in New York, he had been warned the city's music critics had gotten together and agreed "the colored boy has gone far enough." They had decided in advance to give *Troubled Island* bad reviews.

Sure enough, despite the zealous reception that Still's opera received from the public on opening night, Olin Downes of the *New York Times* wrote it was filled with "clichés of Broadway and Hollywood." He said the listener "waits for the lightning flash of genius which has not come," and he hoped Still would be successful in later works. The rest of the New York critics followed Downes's example.

His conductor friend Leopold Stokowski comforted Billy, saying, "This is not the first time I have heard that certain critics write their articles before they listen to the music." Stokowski advised him to be patient. He reminded his friend that it could take time for works of music to be fully appreciated and understood.

There were other consolations as well. The National Association for Composers and Conductors honored Still for his contribution to American music. In addition, the U.S. State Department recorded *Troubled Island* for the Voice of America. This government-funded broadcasting network presents news, educational, and cultural programs to people throughout the world.

Still kept on writing operas, including *Mota* (1951), which was set in Africa, and *Minette Fontaine* (1958), about a nineteenth-century opera star living in New Orleans. Every opera that Still wrote after *Troubled Island* had a libretto by Verna Arvey. "In preparing for an opera, I do the necessary research and outline the plot," Still said. "Then my writer and I get together, and she writes the lines. We work closely together with the text and the music." Sometimes Billy composed music to accompany lyrics that Verna had already written, but more often she tailored her words to fit his melodies. That way, he was free to create music without limiting his imagination. Always handy with tools, Billy built miniature stage sets so that he could visualize the action in his operas.

In 1962, Billy and Verna wrote *Highway 1, U.S.A.*, an opera about an American family that was set in a typically American location, a gas station next to a busy roadway. *Highway 1, U.S.A.* was first performed at the University of Miami in 1963, as part of the school's annual Festival of American Music, and this time the reviews were good. Wrote one music critic, "It is lively, free in spirit, and with a touch of nobility about it."

William Grant Still had turned from seeking inspiration in African-American history and culture to writing music that reflected the wider world. He composed three more symphonies as well as shorter works, including some music for children. In *The Little Song that Wanted to Be a Symphony,* a work for singers and orchestra with narration by Verna Arvey, a melody visits children throughout the United States, teaching brotherhood. As the tune arrives in each community, the orchestra plays it in the style of the people living there. The little song sounds in turn Native American, Cajun, African American, Asian, and Italian, demonstrating every ethnic group has contributed to the sound of American music.

"We'd noticed how children, under natural circumstances, seem to get along so well," Still said. He and Verna had observed, however, that too often as children get older, they learn from their elders to hate and discriminate. "So, the first thought that came to us was how to get the idea of brotherhood . . . over in a musical way to young folks." Still also wrote music to accompany a children's play called *The Prince and the Mermaid.*

As William Grant Still promoted brotherhood through his music, African Americans made important legal gains in the field of civil rights. In 1954, the Supreme Court had ruled that segregated schools violated the rights of African-American children. In 1955 and 1956, a boycott of city buses by the African Americans of Montgomery, Alabama, resulted in a federal court order mandating seating on public transportation without regard for race.

In the spring of 1963, African Americans were on the march in Birmingham, Alabama, to bring integration to the city's downtown shopping area. On August 28, 1963, more than two hundred thousand people showed their commitment to equality in a peaceful demonstration in the nation's capital that was known as the March on Washington. These and other protests helped to secure passage of the Civil Rights Act of 1964, which protected citizens against discrimination in public facilities, schools, and the voting booth.

The Reverend Martin Luther King Jr. emerged as the leader of the nonviolent civil rights movement. He organized the protests in Montgomery and Birmingham. During the March on Washington, he stood on the steps of the Lincoln Memorial to tell the world he dreamed, "one day this nation will rise up and live out the true meaning of its creed—we hold these truths to be self evident that all men are created equal."

By the mid-1960s, though, many young African Americans had grown impatient with King's leadership and the failure of southern communities to abide by the new federal laws. Young militants were eager to enforce "Black Power" and bring about immediate social change, using violence if necessary. At the same time, a powerful religious and political group, the Nation of Islam, called for separation of the races and urged African

Americans to depend on themselves alone.

Still had spent his working life trying to bring people together, and he rejected the inflammatory talk of the militants. "To all those who talk of separation, I would say again that I am now and forever against it. I'm for integration," he said. "We're all Americans in our hearts, in our music, in our very being."

Billy and Verna visited schools to talk to children about music, and they found pleasure in their growing family. Duncan was pursuing a career as a nuclear engineer. Judith Anne, who studied English in college, had married Larry Headlee, a geologist. Between 1963 and 1969, Judith and Larry had a son and three daughters. When these grandchildren came to visit, Billy joyfully cried out, "Verna, come quick! The babies are here!" The children played with the toys and puzzles that their grandfather had made for Judith and Duncan when they were small.

In later life, William Grant Still enjoyed the reputation he had long deserved. He became known as the "Dean of Afro-American Composers" for his outstanding contributions to music for the concert hall. Writing about Still, a New Orleans newspaper reporter commented, "He broke barriers of race in symphonic music, not through revolution, but by gentle, attractive persuasion." Some of the most important orchestras in the world performed Still's work, and he received many requests to write music, conduct, or speak.

At the University of California at Los Angeles, for example, he lectured about the need for composers of all races and nationalities to have their music heard. "God didn't place only roses on earth, or only lilies or only violets," he said. "He put flowers of many sorts and many colors here, the beauty of each enhancing that of the others. Anyone who underestimates the great value of differences would do well to remember that life would indeed be dull without variety. Progress would be impossible if all thought alike."

On November 9, 1970, the orchestra at Oberlin introduced Still's *Symphony No. 5,* which is subtitled "Western Hemisphere." In its four movements, this symphony portrays the abundance of North and South America, the natural beauty of the two continents, the vigor of their people, and the spirit of kindness and fairness that envelops the hemisphere.

Still's golden years were contented ones, but tragedies can occur during the happiest times. In 1970, he and Verna were devastated to learn their beloved son-in-law, Larry Headlee, had died. Larry had been aboard a small submarine in the waters off California when it was involved in an accident, and he had been killed. The bad news was a blow to Billy both mentally and physically, and four months after Larry's funeral, he suffered a heart attack and stroke and was left permanently weak.

Nevertheless, people commented he looked like a man of fifty, and he continued to be honored and to appear in public. He received honorary degrees—eight in all—from schools such as the University of Arkansas, the New England Conservatory of Music, and

William Grant Still and Mississippi Governor William Lowe Waller at the ceremony naming Still "a distinguished Mississippian," in 1974. *(Courtesy of the University of Arkansas.)*

Oberlin Conservatory. In 1974, he was named a Distinguished Mississippian by Governor William Lowe Waller of Mississippi, the state where he was born.

In 1975, the University of Southern California Friends of Music held a banquet in honor of William Grant Still's eightieth birthday. Surrounded by loved ones and admirers, the composer listened to a speech by his old friend Howard Hanson. Hanson talked about his long acquaintance with Still and the premier of the *First Symphony* in 1931. "Here was a symphony in the conventional four movements, beautifully constructed . . .

but yet with a new ingredient never before seen," Hanson said. It was not just "an American symphony, but it was an Afro-American symphony." Hanson recalled for his listeners the 1933 concert in Berlin at which the audience demanded two repetitions of the third movement of the *Afro-American Symphony*. "I doubt if that has ever happened in Berlin before or since," Hanson said.

He went on to praise Still, calling him "a gentle man," and a person of "simplicity, friendship, love and beauty."

Later that year, Still accepted an honorary degree from the University of Southern California. It was to be his last public appearance. A series of heart attacks and strokes soon left him in need of constant medical care, and he spent his last years in a nursing home. He died on December 3, 1978, at eighty-three years of age.

In June 1969, while attending a seminar on African-American music at Indiana University, William Grant Still was asked what music meant to him. He replied, "To state it in the simplest terms, for me, music is beauty." Through his operas, symphonies, and shorter works, he furthered racial harmony and made the world a more beautiful place.

Major Works

Music for the Orchestra
Darker America (1924)
From the Land of Dreams (1925)
Africa (1928)
Afro-American Symphony (1930)
Symphony in G Minor, "Song of a New Race" (1937)
In Memoriam: The Colored Soldiers Who Died for Democracy
   (1943)
Fanfare for the 99th Fighter Squadron (1945)
Symphony No. 5, "Western Hemisphere" (1945)
Symphony No. 4, "Autochthonous" (1947)
Symphony No. 3, "The Sunday Symphony" (1958)

Ballets
La Guiablesse (1927)
Sahdji (1930)

Operas
Blue Steel (1934)
Troubled Island (1941)
Costaso (1950)

Mota (1951)
Minette Fontaine (1958)
Highway 1, U.S.A. (1962)

Songs and Choral Works
Levee Land (1925)
Lenox Avenue (1937)
And They Lynched Him on a Tree (1940)
Plain Chant for America (1940)
The Little Song that Wanted to Be a Symphony (1954)

Timeline

1895   On May 11, William Grant Still Jr. is born in Woodville, Mississippi; three months later, William Grant Still Sr. dies; Carrie Still and Will move to Little Rock, Arkansas.

1906   Carrie Still marries Charles B. Shepperson.

1911   William finishes high school and enters Wilberforce University in Ohio.

1915   Leaves Wilberforce shortly before graduation; marries Grace Bundy on October 4.

1916   Grace moves to Danville, Kentucky, in May; in summer, W.C. Handy hires Will; a son, William Bundy Still, is born in November.

1917   Still receives an inheritance from his father; enrolls in the Oberlin Conservatory of Music; serves in the navy during World War I.

1918   A second child, Gail Linton Still, is born.

1919   Still returns briefly to Oberlin; moves to Manhattan; works for the Pace and Handy Music Company.

1920   A daughter, June Allen Still, is born.

1922   Travels to Boston with a road company of *Shuffle Along;* studies composition with George W. Chadwick;

subsequently is employcd by Black Swan Records.

1923   Begins study with Edgard Varèse.

1924   The fourth child, Caroline Elaine Still, is born.

1925   *From the Land of Dreams* is performed in a concert sponsored by the International Composers' Guild.

1926   *Levee Land* is performed at New York's Aeolian Hall, featuring Florence Mills; *Darker America* is included in a concert at the Eastman School of Music in Rochester, New York.

1927   On May 18, Carrie Shepperson dies; Still receives the story "Sahdji" from Alain Locke.

1928   Wins an award from the Harmon Foundation.

1929   Travels to Los Angeles to arrange songs for radio.

1930   Returns to New York City; on October 30, begins composing the *Afro-American Symphony.*

1931   On May 22, *Sahdji* becomes the first ballet to be performed in concert at the Eastman School of Music; on October 28, the *Afro-American Symphony* is presented in Rochester; Still becomes an arranger for Willard Robison's "Deep River Hour."

1932   Grace Still moves to Canada with the couple's four children.

1933   *La Guiablesse* is performed in Rochester.

1934   *La Guiablesse* is presented in Chicago, featuring Katherine Dunham; Still wins a Guggenheim Fellowship and moves to Los Angeles to compose an opera, *Blue Steel.*

1936   Works briefly for Columbia Pictures; on July 23, conducts the Los Angeles Philharmonic Orchestra at the Hollywood Bowl.

1937   Begins composing *Troubled Island; Lenox Avenue* is broadcast on May 22; Leopold Stokowski and the Philadelphia Orchestra perform the *Symphony in G Minor.*

1939   After divorcing Grace, Still marries Verna Arvey on

February 8; on April 30, the New York World's Fair opens with theme music composed by William Grant Still.

1940 Duncan Allan Still is born; Still composes *And They Lynched Him on a Tree,* which on June 25 is performed in New York and broadcast on the radio.

1941 Still sets to music *Plain Chant for America,* which is performed in London on October 23.

1942 On August 31, Judith Anne Still is born.

1943 Still composes *In Memoriam: The Colored Soldiers Who Died for Democracy.*

1945 Composes *Fanfare for the 99th Fighter Squadron.*

1949 On March 31, *Troubled Island* is performed for the first time at the New York City Center for Music and Drama.

1951 Still composes the opera *Mota,* with a libretto by Verna Arvey.

1958 Still and Arvey write *Minette Fontaine.*

1963 The opera *Highway 1, U.S.A.* is debuted at Miami University.

1970 On November 9, Still's *Symphony No. 5* is presented at the Oberlin Conservatory; son-in-law, Larry Headlee, dies in a submarine accident.

1974 The governor of Mississippi names Still a Distinguished Mississippian.

1975 The University of Southern California Friends of Music mark Still's eightieth birthday with a banquet; Still accepts from the University of Southern California his eighth and final honorary degree; a series of heart attacks and strokes require him to move to a nursing home.

1978 William Grant Still dies on December 3.

Sources

EPIGRAPH

p. 5, "nothing ever is . . ." Robert Bartlett Haas, ed., *William Grant Still and the Fusion of Cultures in American Music* (Los Angeles: Black Sparrow Press, 1972), 53.

CHAPTER ONE: The Teacher's Child

p. 9, "Little David, play on your harp . . ." R. Nathaniel Dett, ed., *Religious Folk-Songs of the Negro as Sung at Hampton Institute* (Hampton, Va.: Hampton Institute Press, 1927), 64.

p. 9, "*must* amount to something . . ." Catherine Parsons Smith, *William Grant Still: A Study in Contradictions* (Berkeley: University of California Press, 2000), 320.

p. 10, "When we all awaken . . ." Gayle Murchison, " 'Dean of Afro-American Composers' or 'Harlem Renaissance Men,' " in Smith, *William Grant Still,* 59.

p. 14, "horrified me . . ." William Grant Still, "My Arkansas Boyhood." *Arkansas Historical Quarterly,* Autumn 1967, 286.

p. 14, "An American, in the finest sense . . ." Judith Anne Still, "Carrie Still Shepperson: The Hollows of Her Footsteps." *Arkansas Historical Quarterly,* Spring 1983, 41.

p. 14, "the path of least resistance . . ." Verna Arvey, *In One Lifetime* (Fayetteville: University of Arkansas Press, 1984), 25.

p. 14, "She had an educated whipping strap . . ." Ibid., 39.

p. 16, "The thought that I was 'hearing authentic Negro music . . ." William Grant Still, "My Arkansas Boyhood," 289.

p. 17, "There is little or no opposition . . ." Louis R. Harlan and Raymond W. Smock, eds., *The Booker T. Washington Papers*. Vol. 8: *1904-6* (Urbana: University of Illinois Press, 1979), 441.

CHAPTER TWO: Nothing but Music

p. 24, "No more beautiful or suitable place . . ." Horace Talbert, *Sons of Allen* (Xenia, Oh.: Aldine Press, 1906), 267.

p. 25, "patriotism is more staunchly developed . . ." Ibid., 278.

p. 26, "Are you at it again?" Arvey, *In One Lifetime,* 38.

p. 27, "They certainly didn't think I was great . . ." Ibid.

p. 28, "I *must* become a composer." William Grant Still, "My Arkansas Boyhood," 291.

p. 29, "And so I wasted time . . ." William Grant Still, "Personal Notes," in Smith, *William Grant Still,* 217.

p. 30, "Nothing but music would do." William Grant Still, "My Arkansas Boyhood," 291.

p. 33, "This was a promise . . ." Ibid.

CHAPTER THREE: Restless

p. 34, "I hate to see that evenin' sun go down . . ." W.C. Handy, "The St. Louis Blues," 1914.

p. 34, "Southern Negroes sang about everything . . ." W.C. Handy, *Father of the Blues* (New York: Macmillan, 1944), 74.

p. 35, "A yearning for unattainable happiness." Murchison, " 'Dean of Afro-American Composers,' " in Smith, *William Grant Still,* 55.

p. 35, "I learned . . . to appreciate . . ." Ibid.

p. 36, "The lark is silent in his nest . . ." Paul Laurence Dunbar, "Good-Night," in *The Complete Poems of Paul Laurence Dunbar* (New York: Dodd, Mead and Co., 1913), 61.

p. 37, "I told him that . . ." William Grant Still, "Personal Notes," in Smith, *William Grant Still,* 218.

CHAPTER FOUR: New York

p. 46, "Now wait. Hold it." Judith Anne Still, ed., *William Grant Still: An Oral History* (Flagstaff, Ariz.: The Master-Player Library, 1998), 17.

p. 48, "Don't get soft!" Arvey, *In One Lifetime,* 65.

p. 48, "I was so nervous . . ." William Grant Still, "Personal Notes," in Smith, *William Grant Still,* 222.

p. 48, "Mr. Still has a very sensuous . . ." Ibid., 222-23.

p. 49, "an incoherent fantasy . . ." Ibid., 222.

p. 49, "the rollicking and often original . . ." Ibid., 222.

p. 49, "It is not Still but Varèse . . ." Ibid., 223.

p. 50, "finding a new soul." Alain Locke, *The New Negro* (New York: Atheneum, 1992), xxvii.

p. 51, "There is a renewed race-spirit . . ." Ibid.

p. 52, "These works are so good, healthy . . ." William Grant Still, "Personal Notes," in Smith, *William Grant Still,* 224.

p. 53, "Where can we find another . . ." Arvey, *In One Lifetime,* 69.

p. 53, "intended to suggest . . ." Carol J. Oja, *Making Music Modern: New York in the 1920s* (New York: Oxford University Press, 2000), 345.

p. 53, "the people seem about . . ." Ibid.

p. 53, "enabling the hearers to form . . ." Block, Maxine, ed., *Current Biography 1941* (New York: H. W. Wilson Co., 1941), 364.

p. 55, "I'm going to use it . . ." Judith Anne Still, ed., *An Oral History,* 16.

p. 55, "would sit there . . ." Smith, *William Grant Still,* 86.

p. 55, "[M]usic is just every bit of me." Judith Anne Still, ed., *An Oral History,* 13.

CHAPTER FIVE: "With Humble Thanks"

p. 56, "Frankly, I would like to see . . ." Murchison, " ' Dean of Afro-American Composers,' " in Smith, *William Grant Still,* 44.

p. 57, "In the heart of the jungle . . ." William Grant Still, *Sahdji: For Ballet, Chorus, and Bass Soloist* (Rochester, N.Y.: Eastman School of Music), 7-8.

p. 57, "Death is at the end . . ." Ibid., 24.

p. 57, "The fig tree does not call . . ." Ibid., 28.

p. 58, "As you know . . ." Miriam Matthews, "Phylon Profile, XXIII: William Grant Still—Composer." *Phylon,* Second Quarter 1951, 110.

p. 58, "This is real music . . ." Smith, *William Grant Still,* 5.

p. 59, "I believe that God . . ." Judith Anne Still, "A Personal Reminiscence of William Grant Still," in *William Grant Still: A Bio-Bibliography,* by Judith Anne Still, Michael J. Dabrishus, and Carolyn L. Quin (Westport, Conn.: Greenwood Press, 1996), 2.

p. 59, "It was not until the depression . . ." Haas, *William Grant Still,* 12.

p. 59, "Things look dark . . ." Smith, *William Grant Still,* 119.

p. 59, "I received some splendid ideas . . ." Ibid.

p. 59, "With humble thanks to God . . ." Matthews, "Phylon Profile," 112.

p. 60, "The symphony has life . . ." William Grant Still, "Personal Notes," in Smith, *William Grant Still,* 231.

p. 61, "Do you see now . . ." Ibid., 232.

p. 61, "The best I ever made." Wayne D. Shirley, "Religion in Rhythm: William Grant Still's Arrangements for Willard Robison's *Deep River Hour." Black Music Research Journal,* Spring 1999, 32.

p. 61, "It is impossible to estimate . . ." Sigmund Spaeth, *A History of Popular Music in America* (New York: Random House, 1948), 478-79.

p. 63, "I stood in the rear . . ." Wayne D. Shirley, ed., "William Grant Still and Irving Schwerke," in Smith, *William Grant Still,* 251.

p. 64, "The music is charming . . ." Verna Arvey, "William Grant Still," in Smith, *William Grant Still,* 325.

p. 65, "I should like to go . . ." Smith, *William Grant Still,* 74.

p. 65, "California did something to me . . ." Judith Anne Still, ed., *An Oral History,* 22.

CHAPTER SIX: Billy

p. 67, "There are no shortcuts . . ." Mary D. Hudgins, "An Outstanding Arkansas Composer: William Grant Still." *Arkansas Historical Quarterly,* Winter 1965, 314.

p. 70, "Please remember that it is absolutely necessary . . ." Smith, *William Grant Still,* 167.

p. 71, "I have a difficult time . . ." Arvey, "William Grant Still," in Smith, *William Grant Still,* 333.

p. 71, "Just as the spark . . ." Haas, *William Grant Still,* 100.

p. 72, "It may be said . . ." Murchison, " 'Dean of Afro-American Composers,' " in Smith, *William Grant Still,* 53.

p. 74, "Our wagon is hitched . . ." Larry Zim, Mel Lerner, and Herbert Rolfes, *The World of Tomorrow: The 1939 New York World's Fair* (New York: Harper & Row, 1988), 9.

p. 74, "I must admit . . ." Smith, *William Grant Still,* 74.

p. 74, "As for myself . . ." Arvey, *In One Lifetime,* 106.

p. 76, "We have had a barrage . . ." Smith, *William Grant Still,* 164.

p. 76, "didn't marry because we wanted . . ." Mr. and Mrs. William Grant Still, "Does Interracial Marriage Succeed?" *Negro Digest,* April 1945, 50.

p. 76, "If a marriage succeeds . . ." Ibid.

CHAPTER SEVEN: Family Man

p. 77, "Gee, but I love those kids . . ." William Grant Still, "Personal Notes," in Smith, *William Grant Still,* 218.

p. 78, "as long as we had a roof . . ." Arvey, *In One Lifetime,* 112.

p. 78, "The sounds of slowly evolving chords . . ." Judith Anne Still, "In My Father's House . . ." *The Black Perspective in Music,* May 1975, 201.

p. 78, "Those were very happy years . . ." Eileen Southern, "Conversation With . . . William Grant Still." *The Black Perspective in Music,* May 1975, 172.

p. 80, "We've swung him higher . . ." *And They Lynched Him on a Tree,* poem by Katherine Garrison Chapin, music by William Grant Still. Musical score in the collection of the Library of Congress, N.p, N.d., 2-3.

p. 80, "Oh my God . . ." Ibid., 20.

p. 80, "Oh sorrow, oh sorrow . . ." Ibid., 24.

p. 80, "He was a man." Ibid., 36.

p. 80, "It is not given to many . . ." Arvey, *In One Lifetime,* 116.

p. 81, "a hemisphere darkens . . ." *Plain Chant for America,* poem by Katherine Garrison Chapin, music by William Grant Still. Musical score in the collection of the Library of Congress, N.p., N.d., 6.

p. 81, "No dark signs close the doors . . ." Ibid., 12-13.

p. 83, "Our civilization has known . . ." Matthews, "Phylon Profile," 107.

p. 83, "come back to a better world." Ibid. 107-108.

p. 84, "with sympathy and feeling . . ." Haas, *William Grant Still,* 149.

p. 84, "says what it has to say . . ." Ibid.

p. 85, "When he was not writing music . . ." Judith Anne Still, "A Personal Reminiscence," 11.

p. 85, "This opera is the dream . . ." Carolyn L. Quin, "Biographical Sketch of William Grant Still," in Still, Dabrishus, and Quin, 37.

p. 86, "The City Center is humming . . ." Ibid.

p. 86, "sounds very lovely indeed . . ." Ibid.

p. 86, "I remember how he looked . . ." Judith Anne Still, "In My Father's House," 203.

p. 86, "Well, Verna . . ." Ibid.

CHAPTER EIGHT: "Music is Beauty"

p. 87, "the colored boy . . ." Smith, *William Grant Still,* 193.

p. 87, "clichés of Broadway . . ." Olin Downes, "Halasz Presents New Still Opera." *New York Times,* April 1, 1949, 30.

p. 87, "waits for the lightning flash . . ." Ibid.

p. 87, "This is not the first time . . ." Quin, "Biographical Sketch," 37.

p. 88, "In preparing for an opera . . ." Southern, "Conversation," 173.

p. 89, "It is lively . . ." Quin, "Biographical Sketch," 39.

p. 89, "We'd noticed how children . . ." Judith Anne Still, "A Personal Reminiscence," 12.

p. 89, "So, the first thought . . ." Ibid., 12-13.

p. 90, "one day this nation . . ." "Excerpts from Addresses at the Lincoln Memorial During Capital Civil Rights March." *New York Times,* August 29, 1963, C21.

p. 91, "To all those who talk . . ." "William Grant Still." *Classical Music Hall of Fame.* URL: http://www.classichall.org/bio1.asp?1name=still Downloaded August 25, 2002.

p. 91, "Verna, come quick!" Judith Anne Still, "A Personal Reminiscence," 13.

p. 91, "Dean of Afro-American Composers," Quin, "Biographical Sketch," 40.

p. 91, "He broke barriers . . ." Arvey, *In One Lifetime,* 183.

p. 92, "God didn't place only roses . . ." Haas, *William Grant Still,* 113.

p. 93, "Here was a symphony . . ." "William Grant Still." *Classical Music Hall of Fame.*

p. 93, "I doubt if that has ever . . ." Ibid.

p. 93, "a gentle man," Judith Anne Still, *William Grant Still,* 14.

p. 94, "simplicity, friendship . . ." Ibid.

p. 94, "To state it in the simplest . . ." Southern, "Conversation," 165.

Bibliography

Arvey, Verna. *In One Lifetime.* Fayetteville: University of Arkansas Press, 1984.

Dett, R. Nathaniel. *Religious Folk-Songs of the Negro as Sung at Hampton Institute.* Hampton, Va.: Hampton Institute Press, 1927.

Francis, David W. and Diane De Mali Francis. *Luna Park: Cleveland's Fairyland of Pleasure.* Fairview Park, Oh.: Amusement Park Books, 1996.

Haas, Robert Bartlett. *William Grant Still and the Fusion of Cultures in American Music.* Los Angeles: Black Sparrow Press, 1972.

Handy, W. C. *Father of the Blues.* New York: Macmillan, 1944.

Harlan, Louis R. and Raymond W. Smock, eds. *The Booker T. Washington Papers.* Vol. 8: *1904-6.* Urbana: University of Illinois Press, 1979.

Hudgins, Mary D. "An Outstanding Arkansas Composer: William Grant Still." *Arkansas Historical Quarterly* 24, no. 4 (Winter 1965).

Matthews, Miriam. "Phylon Profile XXIII: William Grant Still—Composer." *Phylon* 12, no. 2 (Second Quarter 1951).

Oja, Carol J. *Making Music Modern: New York in the 1920s.* New York: Oxford University Press, 2000.

Richards, Ira Don. "Little Rock on the Road to Reunion. 1865-1880." *Arkansas Historical Quarterly* 25, no. 4 (Winter 1966).

Smith, Catherine Parsons. *William Grant Still: A Study in Contradictions.* Berkeley: University of California Press, 2000.

Southern, Eileen. "Conversation with . . .William Grant Still." *The Black Perspective in Music,* May 1975.

Still, Judith Anne. "Carrie Still Shepperson: The Hollows of Her Footsteps." *Arkansas Historical Quarterly* 42, no. 1 (Spring 1983).

_____. "In My Father's House . . ." *The Black Perspective in Music,* May 1975, 199-206.

Still, Judith Anne, ed. *William Grant Still: An Oral History.* Flagstaff, Ariz.: The Master-Player Library, 1998.

Still, Judith Anne, Michael J. Dabrishus, and Carolyn L. Quin. *William Grant Still: A Bio-Bibliography.* Westport, Conn.: Greenwood Press, 1996.

Still, William Grant. "Can Music Make a Career?" *Negro Digest* 7, no. 2 (December 1948).

_____. "The Men Behind American Music." *Crisis* 51, no. 1 (January 1944).

Still, William Grant, as told to Verna Arvey. "My Arkansas Boyhood." *Arkansas Historical Quarterly* 26, no. 3 (Autumn 1967).

Still, William Grant, and Verna Arvey. "Does Interracial Marriage Succeed?" *Negro Digest* 3, no. 6 (April 1945).

Websites

Duke University, "Still Going On: An Exhibit Celebrating the Life and Times of William Grant Still"
http://scriptorium.lib.duke.edu/sgo/

University of Arkansas, William Grant Still and Verna Arvey Papers
http://www.uark.edu/libinfo/speccoll/still/still1aid.html

Harlem Renaissance
http://www.africana.com/Articles/tt_387.htm

Index